Summary & Analysis of Let Us Dream

By Pope Francis

Samantha Evans

DEDICATION

To Alan

Love you now and always!

TABLE OF CONTENTS

INTRODUCTION

The book *Let Us Dream* is a book of encouragement and hope, one that strengthens us in whatever area we may need help in. Born as a response to the needs of members around the pandemic, it has truly served more than that purpose and can be used to weather any storm we might be facing.

The book captures his response to the crisis. It is motivational and inspirational and gives the reader and individuals hope that although life might inevitably be a pain in the ass, it's the little things, our friends and family that make life pretty awesome.

Enjoy,

KEY INSIGHTS AND TAKEAWAYS

As our valued reader, you are important to us. We cherish your Time and Focus. While reading we captured the essential learning points to create an effective mental map of the book and to better remember the vital areas of the book applicable to life.

1. Overcoming crisis and trials:

This book centers on crisis; its effects, the solutions and our response to it. The pandemic has brought changes and challenges that no one was prepared for; Losses, deaths, pains, challenges and many negative occurrences came along with the pandemic.

Currently, many are yet to fully adapt to this present change, we find out that we are faced with also the difficulty of choice. But the basic rule of crisis is that you don't come out of it the same. If you get through it, you come out better or worse, but never the same.

The author tells us stories of hope, around the world and also shares with us Scriptures to remind us who we are in Christ (*1 Peter 2:10*) and God's eternal love for every one of us. He doesn't relent in encouraging our hearts to stand firm and united through the face of crisis. And furthermore, through this book he shares with us his experiences, and facts which points us towards the possibility of Hope for a better future.

2. Living a life full of Service, love and Sacrifice

This theme is thoroughly emphasized all through this book. According to the Author *"We need a movement of people who know we need each other, who have a sense of responsibility to others and to the world."*

The Author emphasizes the need to express love and offer service in all areas and aspect of life. Love is the only factor that brings unity amongst different set of people. This is possible when we all desire to help and make sacrifices on behalf of others. Living a life full of service and love, according to the Author,

> *"Reminds us that our lives are a gift and we grow by giving of ourselves: not preserving ourselves, but losing ourselves in service."*

And as a people and church we ought to offer service to men as Christ did

3. Keeping our hearts open to learn

To make any change at all, our hearts must be open to learn. We must be willing to rely on the spirit of God for directions and discernment when faced with questions, worries and uncertainty.

Crisis and trials can open our minds to various possibilities and even options, some right and some bad. How then can we make the right choice? The answers we need can be known by the Spirit, but we need to open our hearts, be willing to rely on and trust God.

4. Value

According to the Author *"A crisis is almost always the result of a self-forgetting, and the way forward comes through recalling our roots."*

The time of crisis is a time to recover values, in the proper sense of the word: to return to what is authentically worthwhile. The value of life, of nature, of the dignity of the person, of work, of relationship— all these are values key to human life, which cannot be traded away or sacrificed.

5. The need for discernment over fundamentalism

"Coronavirus has accelerated a change of era that was already under way…we are now living through, and what we once considered normal will increasingly no longer be. It is an illusion to think that we can go back to where we were."

The book defines Fundamentalism as the means of assembling thoughts and behavior as a refuge that supposedly protects a person from crisis. Fundamentalist mindsets offers to shelter people from destabilizing situations in exchange for a kind of existential quietism. It offers an attitude and a single close way of thinking as a substitute for the kind of thinking that opens one up to the truth. And this is very dangerous as it makes one afraid of setting out on the road to truth.

Discernment on the other hand, helps us to navigate through situations as we seek the truth, and truth reveals itself to anyone who opens herself to it.

6. The need for Fraternity over individualism

The book defines Fraternity as the sense of belonging to each other and to the whole of humanity. It is the capacity to work and come together against a shared horizon of possibilities. It entails cooperation among a wide range of individuals with differences.

In the Jesuit tradition, it is called the Union of hearts and minds. It's a unity that allows people serve as a body despite differences of viewpoint, physical separation, and human ego. Such a union preserves and respects plurality, inviting all to contribute from their distinctiveness, as a community of brothers and sisters concerned for each other.

The world sorely needs this kind of unity. The pandemic has exposed the paradox that while we are interconnected we are also divided. Fraternity is a step towards change.

Individualism on the other hand, speaks solely of self, it entails selfishness and indifference. And if we desire a change it is necessary to understand the power of a consolidated effort towards a goal as opposed to an individualistic approach.

7. A sign of hope In the midst of hopelessness

When faced with crisis or feelings of hopelessness, what we need at that moment is a sign of hope. A sign is something that stands out and strikes us. According to the Pope

"When faced with difficult times, I take hope from the last words of Jesus in Matthew's Gospel: "I am with you always, to the end of the age" (**Matthew 28:20).**

We are not alone. That is why we need not be afraid to go down into the dark nights of problems and suffering. We know that we don't have the answers all ready and neatly packaged, yet we trust that the Lord will open for us doors we had no idea were there.

One of the signs of hope that the author highlights in this book is the leading role of women. Women across the globe are being given the opportunity to exhibit exceptional leadership even in the Vatican City. This is proof of the possibility of a change towards a better future.

8. The Obstacles to Change

"Let's consider a big obstacle to change, the existential myopia that allows us defensively to select what we see." Pope Francis

Our present day culture is one full of indifference and selfishness. Everyone only sees his/her immediate need and how to solve it. We select what we want to see, but, little did we know that this would be an obstacle to the positive change we desire.

The author mentions three disastrous ways through which we block growth and our connection with reality. They are- Narcissism, Discouragement, and Pessimism.

In our attempt to see only what concerns us, we in turn act negatively towards others. The attitude of God on the other hand is completely different, God is never indifferent. And according to the Author

"The essence of God is mercy, which is not just seeing and being moved, but responding with action. God knows, feels, and comes running out to look for us. He doesn't just wait. Whenever in the world you have a response that is immediate, close, warm, and concerned, offering a response, that's where God's Spirit is present."

9. Solidarity

"If we are to come out of this crisis better, we have to recover the knowledge that as a people we have a shared destination. The pandemic has reminded us that no one is saved alone".

The Pope reminds us that truly no man stands alone, and what ties us to each other is what we commonly call solidarity. In this book we are reminded of the fact that solidarity is more than acts of generosity, as important as it is. Solidarity is a call to embrace the reality that we are bound by bonds of reciprocity. And with this knowledge we can be able to build a better, different, and human future.

SUMMARY OF CHAPTERS

PART I

A Time to See

Pope Francis in this chapter, expresses his thoughts, heart pains, and goodwill message of hope to every individual, families, group and country that has experienced loses, pains, discrimination, poverty, and hopelessness, during this pandemic crisis. He recalls the time he spent alone during the lockdown, times he spent dutifully offering up prayers and help to all those in need. He acknowledges this moment and in his words he expresses his state of heart towards everyone.

"IN THIS PAST YEAR OF change and, my mind and heart have overflowed with people… there are so many places of ceaseless conflict, there's so much suffering and need. I find it helps to focus on concrete situations: you see faces looking for life and love in the reality of each person, of each people. You see hope written in the story of every nation, glorious because it's a story of sacrifice, of daily struggle, of lives broken in self-sacrifice. So rather than overwhelm you, it invites you to ponder, and to respond with hope."

He goes on and lays further emphasis on the theme "**Helping and sacrifice**". He grieves the individuals that lost their lives while they sacrificially offered help to others.

According to The Pope, this service of love reminds us that our lives are a gift and we grow by giving of ourselves: not preserving ourselves, but losing ourselves in service. And with a clear message of hope, he draws out our hearts to the recollection of the fact that we are born, beloved creatures of our Creator, God of love, into a world that has lived long before us. We belong to God and to one another, and we are part of creation. And from this understanding, grasped by the heart must flow our love for each other.

In his message he speaks on moments when we may feel a radical powerlessness that we cannot escape on our own, and tags it as a point where we actually come to see the selfishness of the culture we are immersed in. He encourages us with the words of the Bible, to rely on God's word of love towards us.

Pope Francis goes further on, and highlights three disastrous things that can hinder us from facing reality and walking in love and service to all. They are: Narcissism, discouragement, Pessimism. According to him "these are three ways that block you, paralyze you, and cause you to focus on those things that stop you from moving ahead. They are all in the end about preferring the illusions that mask reality rather than discovering all we might be able to achieve."

According to the Pope, Covid has unmasked another pandemic, and on a daily basis the selfishness of man is revealed, in other words, the word "existential myopia" becomes more profound. And the solution to this will be the word "Change". We must therefore all begin to dream of a real change, a change that is possible. Most importantly, we must never lose sight of the will of God, in all situations and crisis we must be willing to take the words of Jesus, and bear in our hearts that he is always with us.

In regards to the negative effects of the pandemic, he made mention of the sacrifices and suffering that came alongside the pandemic; the negative vices and the expressions of violence and abuse, the disheartening encounters and stories of people he has met. He refers strongly to indifference, selfishness of men and so on as the causes of the evils of the world. He strongly affirms the need for a heart of love, service and sacrifice. The need for a mindset that is strictly People-Oriented.

At this point, the Pope goes down memory lane, and reveals to us the need for a change. He speaks of the need to focus on redesigning the economy in such a way that it provides for every man a dignified existence. And in explaining his hope for change in this world, the Book of Nehemiah is portrayed in clarity. He refers to the call of Nehemiah and the people's response in agreement, as a movement, an awakening, a rise against those that waged war against them. He sees hope for a change, a new world and system birthed. He sees, above all, the pressing need to strengthen institutions, which are a vital reserve of moral energy and civic love. And in all he encourages us that although we are not there yet, this crisis has revealed a lot and importantly has called forth the sense that we need each other. And now is the time for a new project, a new humanism that can put an end to the globalization of indifference and the hyperinflation of the Individual.

We can work together to achieve it, we can learn what takes us forward, and what sets us back, we can choose

PART II

A Time to Choose

In this chapter the three central ideas in which the book revolves around is revealed. In the first chapter we see the crisis and trials that humanity is faced with. However, this chapter emphasizes the need to rely on the supernatural for discernment, because, in the face of crisis if we are going to make a change towards a better future, we have to see clearly, choose well and act right.

According to the Pope Francis "Discernment means to think through our decisions and actions, not just by rational calculation but by listening for His Spirit, recognizing in prayer God's motives, invitations, and will."

Discernment, according to the Pope is an essential step in facing the prevailing crisis. Discernment aids us in making the right decision towards a better future. Discernment by the Spirit will be our guide into all truth.

Times of Crisis are points in our lives where we are faced with a lot of options, challenges and lots of questions. In the face of these questions for instance ("The disruption of Covid has turned the tables, inviting us to stop, alter our routines and priorities, and to ask: What if the economic, the social, and the ecological challenges we face are really different faces of the same crisis?) Our answer and response to this questions in our heart, is in discernment by the

13

Spirit, and this answer is open to us when we humbly search, listen, reflect and pray.

Also, when we discern what is and what is not of God, we begin to see where and how to act.

The Pope goes further to open our eyes towards a positive occurrence, a Sign of Hope . He defines a sign as something that "stands out and strikes us". And the sign of hope in this crisis is the leading role of women. He goes down memory lane and highlights key situations and examples where women have proven themselves as exceptional leaders and great thinkers. He intentionally speaks on the integration of the view points of women, the need to open up and allow them room to project their ideas. He explains his desire and the conscious effort he has put into creating spaces where women can lead, but in ways that allow them to shape the culture, ensuring that they are valued, respected, and recognized.

Another view point that the Pope brings into this chapter, is the need to choose between fraternity and individualism as our organizing principle, if we dream of or desire a better future. Fraternity is the sense of belonging to each other and to the whole of humanity. This sense of unity as opposed to individualism allows people to serve despite differences of viewpoint. And in discussing how we can overcome the breaches in our society, to build peace and the common good, the Pope highlights, the need to consider the "isolated conscience". According to the Pope it is important to understand the effect of this bad Spirit, because it closes us in on our own interests and viewpoints by means of suspicion and supposition. In further explanation of the isolated conscience, the Pope reveals its negative effect on individuals and society at large, its causes, ways through which it operates in the hearts of men and finally the solution or antidote.

The Pope finally introduces to us a key point which could help reconcile brewing conflicts and disagreements. In Greek it is called *Synodas* meaning "walking together". And according to Pope Francis, the dynamics of a synod involves the expression and the harmony of differences or disagreement.

"This synodal approach is something our world now needs badly. Rather than seeking confrontation, declaring war, with each side hoping to defeat the other, we need processes that allow differences to be expressed, heard, and left to mature in such a way that we can walk together without needing to destroy anyone."

In conclusion, we learn that discerning in the midst of conflict requires us sometimes to pitch camp together, waiting for the skies to clear. Time belongs to the Lord. And in trusting in Him, we move forward with courage, building unity through discernment.

PART III

A Time to Act

A time of crisis is a time for action, and

"a time for action asks us to recover our sense of belonging, the knowledge that we are part of a people."

The author introduces this chapter with a teaching on unity in the face of crisis. According to him certain calamities are able to awaken a sense of unity, and although it may throw us out of balance, the fact that such calamity can allow people to be awakened, and also initiate a capacity for action is hope.

The pope focuses on the People, what they are, what unites the people, the dignity of the people. The Pope emphasizes on the need for belonging, an awakening and restoration of fraternity and solidarity. According to Pope Francis setting oneself above the people leads to, moralism, legalism, clericalism, pharisaism, and other elitist ideologies.

The Pope points out the role of the Church towards the people, and that is "service towards the people as Christ lived". He speaks further on the needs of the people in all areas, politically, economically, socially. And also the need for government, leaders and all to be people-centric.

According to the Pope the lockdown has opened our eyes to lots of reality that are hidden, he writes on the sufferings of many, injustice, and the value of life. He makes his stand clear against, the death penalty, suicide laws and even on abortion.

Finally, this chapter ends with a call to action, according to the Pope

"It is a mistake to dismiss the Popular Movements as "little" and "local"; that would be to miss their vitality and relevance. They have the potential to revitalize our societies, rescuing them from all that today weakens them."

Concluded

In line with remembering to stay strong and hopeful. Here is a gratitude journal for you to write down things you feel grateful for anytime you happen to be reading this book.

Gratitude Log

What are you thankful for today?

1.

2.

3.

4.

5.

6.

7.

8.

9.

10.

Gratitude Log

What are you thankful for today?

1.

2.

3.

4.

5.

6.

7.

8.

9.

10.

Gratitude Log

What are you thankful for today?

1.

2.

3.

4.

5.

6.

7.

8.

9.

10.

Gratitude Log

What are you thankful for today?

1.

2.

3.

4.

5.

6.

7.

8.

9.

10.

Gratitude Log

What are you thankful for today?

1.

2.

3.

4.

5.

6.

7.

8.

9.

10.

Notes

....
....
....
....
....
....
....
....
....
....
....
....
....
....
....
....
....
....
....
....
....
....
....
....
....
....
....
....
....
....
....

Concluded.

Made in the USA
Monee, IL
18 February 2021